GW00707684

CHRISTMAS FAVOURITES
Playalong *for* Alto Saxophone

Wise Publications
part of The Music Sales Group
London/New York/Paris/Sydney/Copenhagen/Berlin/Madrid/Tokyo

Published by
Wise Publications
8/9 Frith Street, London W1D 3JB, England.

Exclusive Distributors:
Music Sales Limited
Distribution Centre, Newmarket Road, Bury St. Edmunds,
Suffolk IP33 3YB England.
Music Sales Pty Limited
120 Rothschild Avenue, Rosebery, NSW 2018, Australia.

Order No. AM977691
ISBN 1-84449-125-0
This book © Copyright 2003 by Wise Publications.

Compiled by Lucy Holliday.
Music arranged by Simon Lesley.
Music processed by Enigma Music Production Services.
Cover photography by George Taylor.
Printed in Great Britain.

CD recorded, mixed and mastered by Jonas Persson.
Instrumental solos by John Whelan.
Backing tracks by Danny G
(except tracks 5, 7, 15 & 17 by John Maul; and tracks 9 & 19 by Rick Cardinali).

Your Guarantee of Quality:
As publishers, we strive to produce every book to
the highest commercial standards.
The music has been freshly engraved and the book has been
carefully designed to minimise awkward page turns and
to make playing from it a real pleasure.
Particular care has been given to specifying acid-free, neutral-sized
paper made from pulps which have not been elemental chlorine bleached.
This pulp is from farmed sustainable forests and was
produced with special regard for the environment.
Throughout, the printing and binding have been planned to
ensure a sturdy, attractive publication which should give years of enjoyment.
If your copy fails to meet our high standards,
please inform us and we will gladly replace it.

www.musicsales.com

Saxophone Fingering Chart

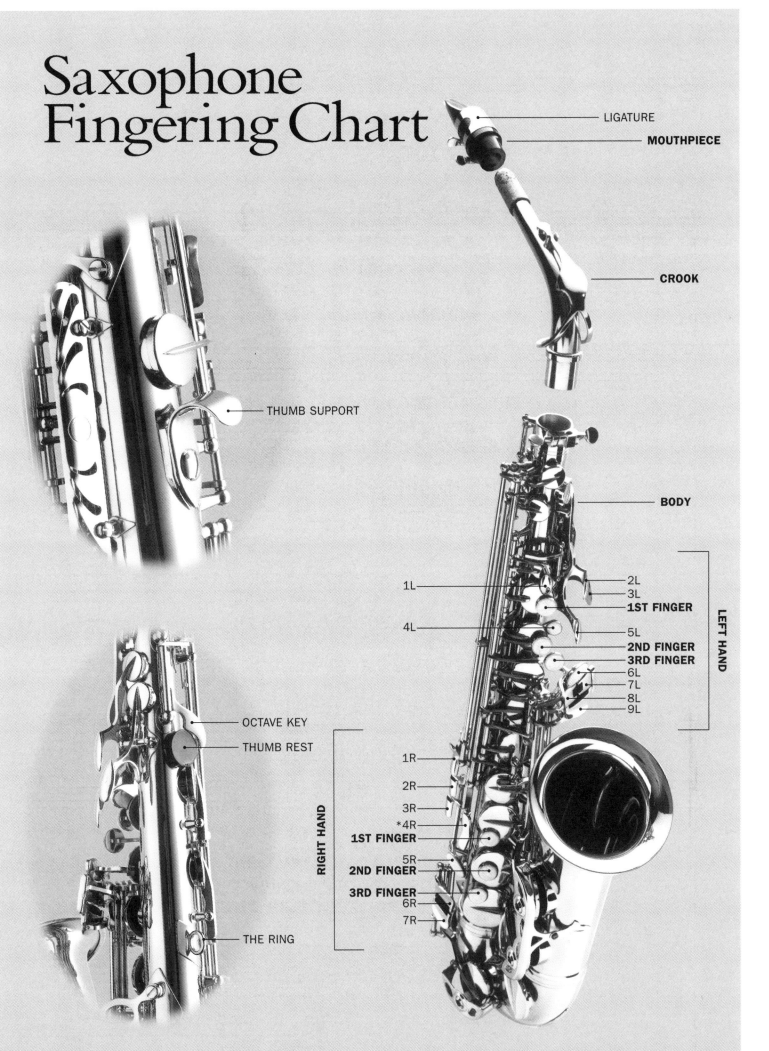

LIGATURE
MOUTHPIECE
CROOK
THUMB SUPPORT
BODY
OCTAVE KEY
THUMB REST
THE RING

1L
2L
3L
1ST FINGER
4L
5L
2ND FINGER
3RD FINGER
6L
7L
8L
9L
LEFT HAND

1R
2R
3R
*4R
1ST FINGER
5R
2ND FINGER
3RD FINGER
6R
7R
RIGHT HAND

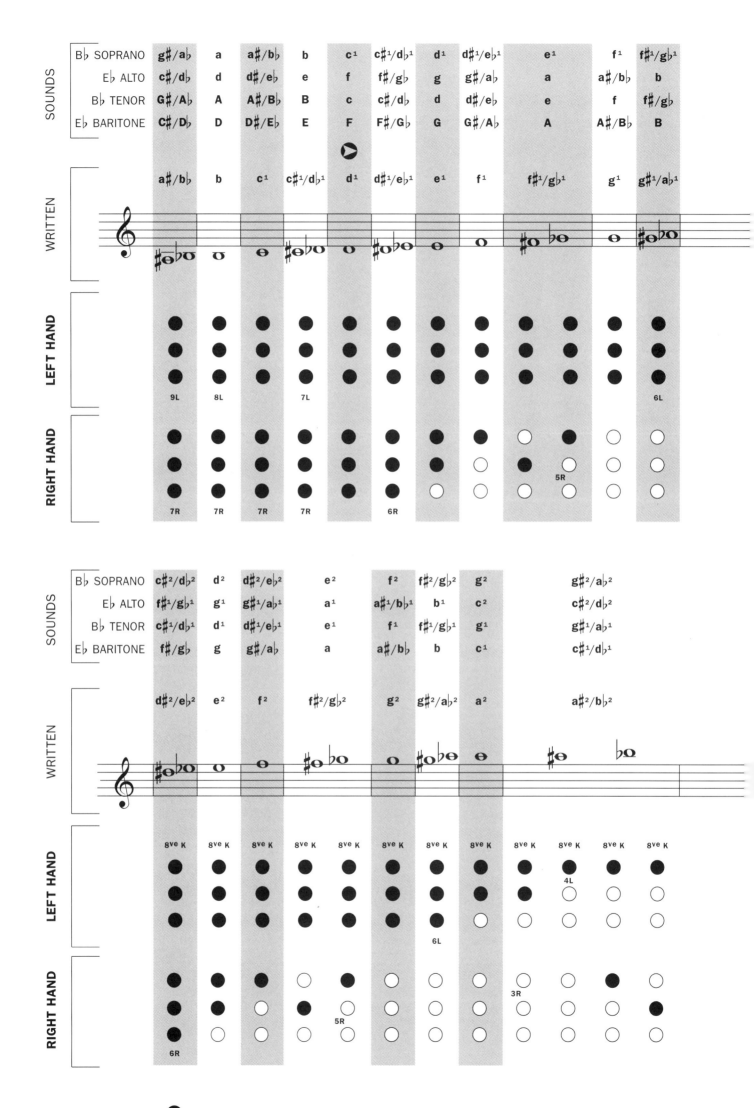

Indicates the lower limit of the best playing range

Indicates the upper limit of the best playing range

Baby, It's Cold Outside

Words & Music by Frank Loesser

Blue Christmas

Words & Music by Billy Hayes & Jay Johnson

C-H-R-I-S-T-M-A-S

Words & Music by Jenny Lou Carson & Eddy Arnold

Lullaby, religioso ♩ = 88

(with backing: strings 8va)

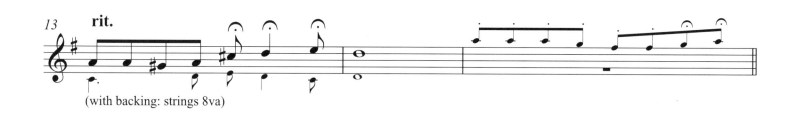

(with backing: strings 16va)

The Christmas Song
(Chestnuts Roasting On An Open Fire)

Words & Music by Mel Torme & Robert Wells

The Christmas Waltz

Words by Sammy Cahn
Music by Jule Styne

Home For The Holidays

Words & Music by Al Stillman & Robert Allen

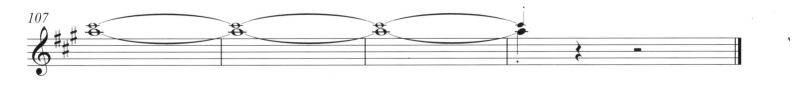

I Saw Mommy Kissing Santa Claus

Words & Music by Tommie Connor

Jingle Bell Rock

Words & Music by Joseph Beal & James Boothe

Let It Snow! Let It Snow! Let It Snow!

Words & Music by Sammy Cahn & Jule Styne

Santa Baby

Words & Music by Joan Javits, Phil Springer & Tony Springer

Put yourself in the spotlight with all these great titles

Now you can have your very own professional backing band...

when you play these superb melody line arrangements
for Clarinet, Flute, Alto Saxophone, Tenor Saxophone*, Trumpet* and Violin*

ABBA
Includes:
Dancing Queen
Fernando
Mamma Mia
Waterloo
AM960905 (Clarinet)
AM960894 (Flute)
AM960916 (Alto Saxophone)
AM960927 (Violin)

BALLADS
Includes:
Candle In The Wind
Imagine
Killing Me Softly With His Song
Wonderful Tonight
AM941787 (Clarinet)
AM941798 (Flute)
AM941809 (Alto Saxophone)

THE BEATLES
Includes:
All You Need Is Love
Hey Jude
Lady Madonna
Yesterday
NO90682 (Clarinet)
NO90683 (Flute)
NO90684 (Alto Saxophone)

CHART HITS
Includes:
Baby One More Time
   (Britney Spears)
Perfect Moment
   (Martine McCutcheon)
That Don't Impress Me Much
   (Shania Twain)
When You Say Nothing At All
   (Ronan Keating)
AM955636 (Clarinet)
AM955647 (Flute)
AM955658 (Alto Saxophone)
AM966724 (Violin)

CHRISTMAS
Includes:
Frosty The Snowman
Have Yourself A Merry Little
   Christmas
Mary's Boy Child
Winter Wonderland
AM950400 (Clarinet)
AM950411 (Flute)
AM950422 (Alto Saxophone)

CHRISTMAS FAVOURITES
Includes:
The Christmas Waltz
Jingle Bell Rock
Let It Snow! Let It Snow! Let It Snow!
Santa Baby
AM977702 (Clarinet)
AM977669 (Flute)
AM977691 (Alto Saxophone)
AM977680 (Violin)

CHRISTMAS HITS
Includes:
Happy Xmas (War Is Over)
   (John Lennon)
Merry Xmas Everybody (Slade)
Mistletoe And Wine
   (Cliff Richard)
Wonderful Christmastime
   (Paul McCartney)
AM966955 (Clarinet)
AM966944 (Flute)
AM966966 (Alto Saxophone)
AM966977 (Violin)

CLASSIC BLUES
Includes:
Fever
Harlem Nocturne
Moonglow
Round Midnight
AM941743 (Clarinet)
AM941754 (Flute)
AM941765 (Alto Saxophone)
AM966702 (Tenor Saxophone)
AM967048 (Trumpet)

CLASSICS
Includes:
Air On The 'G' String – Bach
Jupiter (from The Planets Suite) –
   Holst
Ode To Joy (Theme from
   Symphony No.9 'Choral') –
   Beethoven
Swan Lake (Theme) –
   Tchaikovsky.
AM955537 (Clarinet)
AM955548 (Flute)
AM955560 (Violin)

FILM THEMES
Includes:
Circle Of Life (The Lion King)
Kiss From A Rose
   (Batman Forever)
Moon River
   (Breakfast At Tiffany's)
You Must Love Me (Evita)
AM941864 (Clarinet)
AM941875 (Flute)
AM941886 (Alto Saxophone)

JAZZ
Includes:
Fly Me To The Moon
Opus One
Satin Doll
Straight No Chaser
AM941700 (Clarinet)
AM941710 (Flute)
AM941721 (Alto Saxophone)
AM966779 (Tenor Saxophone)
AM966691 (Trumpet)

LATIN
Includes:
Besame Mucho
Guantanamera
Lambada
Perhaps, Perhaps, Perhaps
AM966064 (Clarinet)
AM966053 (Flute)
AM966075 (Alto Saxophone)
AM967758 (Trumpet)

NEW CHART HITS
Includes:
Colourblind (Darius)
If You're Not The One
   (Daniel Bedingfield)
Love At First Sight
   (Kylie Minogue)
Whenever, Wherever (Shakira)
AM963083 (Clarinet)
AM963061 (Flute)
AM963072 (Alto Saxophone)
AM976855 (Violin)

NEW FILM THEMES
Includes:
A Beautiful Mind
   (All Love Can Be)
Captain Corelli's Mandolin
   (Pelagia's Song)
Crouching Tiger, Hidden Dragon
   (The Eternal Vow)
Moulin Rouge!
   (Come What May)
AM973478 (Clarinet)
AM973489 (Flute)
AM973467 (Alto Saxophone)
AM973500 (Violin)
AM975084 (Cello)

NEW LOVE SONGS
Includes:
Emotion (Destiny's Child)
Evergreen (Will Young)
Hero (Enrique Iglesias)
If You Come Back (Blue)
AM973522 (Clarinet)
AM973533 (Flute)
AM973511 (Alto Saxophone)
AM973544 (Violin)

NINETIES HITS
Includes:
Falling Into You (Celine Dion)
Never Ever (All Saints)
Tears In Heaven (Eric Clapton)
2 Become 1 (Spice Girls)
AM952853 (Clarinet)
AM952864 (Flute)
AM952875 (Alto Saxophone)
AM966713 (Violin)

* selected titles only

No.1 HITS
Includes:
A Whiter Shade Of Pale
  (Procol Harum)
Every Breath You Take
  (The Police)
No Matter What (Boyzone)
Unchained Melody
  (The Righteous Brothers)
AM955603 (Clarinet)
AM955614 (Flute)
AM955625 (Alto Saxophone)
AM959530 (Violin)

SHOWSTOPPERS
Includes:
Big Spender (Sweet Charity)
Bring Him Home (Les Misérables)
I Know Him So Well (Chess)
Somewhere (West Side Story)
AM941820 (Clarinet)
AM941831 (Flute)
AM941842 (Alto Saxophone)

SMASH HITS
Includes:
American Pie (Madonna)
Breathless (The Corrs)
Desert Rose (Sting)
She's The One (Robbie Williams)
AM963040 (Clarinet)
AM963039 (Flute)
AM963050 (Alto Saxophone)
AM968209 (Violin)
AM971157 Trumpet

SOUL
Includes:
I Get The Sweetest Feeling
  (Jackie Wilson)
I Heard It Through The
  Grapevine (Marvin Gaye)
(Sittin' On) The Dock Of The Bay
  (Otis Redding)
Stand By Me (Ben E. King)
AM970200 (Clarinet)
AM970189 (Flute)
AM970211 (Alto Saxophone)
AM970222 (Tenor Saxophone)
AM970233 (Trumpet)

SWING
Includes:
I'm Getting Sentimental
  Over You
Is You Is Or Is You Ain't
  My Baby?
Perdido
Tuxedo Junction
AM949377 (Clarinet)
AM949399 (Alto Saxophone)
AM959618 (Tenor Saxophone)
AM960575 (Trumpet)

TODAY'S HITS
Includes:
Eternal Flame (Atomic Kitten)
Sail Away (David Gray)
Sing (Travis)
What Took You So Long?
  (Emma Bunton)
AM966020 (Clarinet)
AM966010 (Flute)
AM966031 (Alto Saxophone)
AM966042 (Violin)

TV THEMES
Includes:
Black Adder
Home And Away
London's Burning
Star Trek
AM941908 (Clarinet)
AM941919 (Flute),
AM941920 (Alto Saxophone)

Sample the whole series of Guest Spot with these special double CD compilations

GUEST SPOT GOLD
Twenty all-time hit songs, showstoppers and film themes.
Includes:
A Whiter Shade Of Pale
  (Procol Harum)
Bridge Over Troubled Water
  (Simon & Garfunkel)
Don't Cry For Me Argentina
  (from Evita)
Yesterday (The Beatles)
Where Do I Begin
  (Theme from Love Story)
Words (Boyzone)
Yesterday (The Beatles)
AM960729 (Clarinet)
AM960718 (Flute)
AM960730 (Alto Saxophone)

GUEST SPOT PLATINUM
Seventeen great chart hits, ballads and film themes.
Includes:
Circle Of Life (from Walt Disney
  Pictures' The Lion King)
Candle In The Wind (Elton John)
Dancing Queen (ABBA)
Falling Into You (Celine Dion)
I Believe I Can Fly (R. Kelly)
Take My Breath Away (Berlin)
Torn (Natalie Imbruglia)
AM960751 (Clarinet)
AM960740 (Flute)
AM960762 (Alto Saxophone)

20 JAZZ GREATS
Twenty of the best-ever jazz standards.
Includes:
Fever
Fly Me To The Moon
I'm Gettin' Sentimental Over You
Li'l Darlin'
Satin Doll
Take The 'A' Train
AM970453 (Clarinet)
AM970442 (Flute)
AM970464 (Alto Saxophone)
AM970508 (Trumpet)

...and two for two!
Special Duet Editions

GUEST SPOT DUETS GREATEST HITS
Includes:
Angels (Robbie Williams)
It Feels So Good (Sonique)
Livin' La Vida Loca (Ricky Martin)
When You're Gone
  (Bryan Adams and Melanie C)
AM970937 (Clarinet)
AM970926 (Flute)
AM970948 (Alto Saxophone)
AM970959 (Violin)

GUEST SPOT DUETS CHRISTMAS
Includes:
Happy Xmas (War Is Over)
I Wish It Could Be Christmas
  Every Day
Merry Xmas Everybody
Silent Night
AM971927 (Clarinet)
AM971916 (Flute)
AM971938 (Alto Saxophone)
AM971949 (Violin)

Available from all good music retailers or, in case of difficulty, contact
Music Sales Limited,
Newmarket Road, Bury St Edmunds, Suffolk IP33 3YP.
Tel: 01284 725725; Fax: 01284 702592.
www.musicsales.com

Full instrumental performances...

1. Tuning notes
2. Baby, It's Cold Outside
   (Loesser) MPL Communications Ltd.
3. Blue Christmas
   (Hayes/Johnson) Anglo-Pic Music Company Ltd.
4. C-H-R-I-S-T-M-A-S
   (Carson/Arnold) Carlin Music Corp.
5. The Christmas Song
   (Chestnuts Roasting On An Open Fire)
   (Torme/Wells) Chappell-Morris Ltd.
6. The Christmas Waltz
   (Cahn/Styne) Westminster Music Ltd./EMI Music Publishing (WP) Ltd.
7. Home For The Holidays
   (Stillman/Allen) EMI Music Publishing Ltd./Edward Kassner Music Co. Ltd.
8. I Saw Mommy Kissing Santa Claus
   (Connor) Blue Ribbon Music Ltd.
9. Jingle Bell Rock
   (Beal/Boothe) TRO Essex Music Ltd.
10. Let It Snow! Let It Snow! Let It Snow!
    (Cahn/Styne) Cherry Lane Music Ltd.
11. Santa Baby
    (Javits/P. Springer/T. Springer) T.M. Music Ltd.

Backing tracks only...

12. Baby, It's Cold Outside
13. Blue Christmas
14. C-H-R-I-S-T-M-A-S
15. The Christmas Song
    (Chestnuts Roasting On An Open Fire)
16. The Christmas Waltz
17. Home For The Holidays
18. I Saw Mommy Kissing Santa Claus
19. Jingle Bell Rock
20. Let It Snow! Let It Snow! Let It Snow!
21. Santa Baby

To remove your CD from the plastic sleeve, lift the small lip on the right to break the perforated flap. Replace the disc after use for convenient storage.